Gray Whales

DAVID G. GORDON AND ALAN BALDRIDGE

MONTEREY BAY AQUARIUM®

Monterey, California

The purpose of the Monterey Bay Aquarium is to stimulate interest, increase knowledge and promote stewardship of Monterey Bay and the world's ocean environment through innovative exhibits, public education and scientific results.

Acknowledgments   We would like to thank Dr. Marilyn Dahlheim, Dr. Jim Harvey, Dr. Steven K. Webster and Jo Guerrero for their thorough and thoughtful review of the manuscript. Among the many biologists who have written about gray whales, the contributions of R.M. Gilmore, M.L. Jones, D.W. Rice, S.L. Swartz and A.A. Wolman deserve special acknowledgment.

Published in the United States by the Monterey Bay Aquarium Foundation, 886 Cannery Row, Monterey, CA 93940-1085.

Library of Congress Cataloging in Publication Data

Gordon, David G. (David George), 1950-
Gray whales / David G. Gordon and Alan Baldridge.
p.   cm.—(Monterey Bay Aquarium natural history series)
Includes index.
ISBN 1-878244-04-3 : $8.95
1. Gray whale. I. Baldridge, Alan. II. Title. III. Series.
QL737.C425G67 1991
599.5′1—dc20   91-16019 CIP

Photo and Illustration Credits:

Cover: Dugald Stermer
Andrews, Roy/Courtesy American Museum of Natural History: 27
Balthis, Frank S.: 13 (top), 31, 34 (bottom), 60 (top)
Bancroft Library, UC Berkeley: 21, 22, 24 (bottom)
Barrett, Ellie: maps—17, 32, 45, 56
Caudle, Ann: 13 (bottom), 14 (top), 41 (top), 53 (middle right)
Cenzano, Lura/Marine Mammal Images: 10
Clevenger, Ralph: 11 (top left), 43 (right), 48 (top)
Collins, Tia/Marine Mammal Images: 34 (middle)
Collins, Tom/Marine Mammal Images: 14 (bottom)
Cook Photo/Pat Hathaway Collection: 25
Darling, Jim: 42
Folkens, Pieter: 8, 37

Foott, Jeff: 11 (middle), 12 (middle left), 28, 36 (top), 41 (bottom left & right), 43 (left), 61 (top)
Fraker, Mark: 44, 45 (top)
Gohier, Francois: 5, 11 (top right), 12 (top left & right), 35, 38-39
Goodspeed, Ted: 48 (bottom right)
Hall, Howard: 54-55
Harvey, Jim: 9 (bottom), 60 (bottom), 62 (middle)
Hathaway, Pat/Collection: 23
Hillman, Sandra Lynn/ Courtesy of Pacific Grove Natural History Museum Collection: 51
Lanting, Frans/Minden Pictures: 33, 39 (top), 40, 46-47, 57
Martin, Eric/Marine Mammal Images: 1, 47 (top)
McCann, Andrea: 32
Means, Tim/Marine Mammal Images: 61 (bottom)

Miller Library, Hopkins Marine Station, Stanford University: 24 (top), 58
Nicklin, Flip/Nicklin & Associates: 49, 50
Ormsby, Lawrence: 6-7
San Francisco Maritime NHP: 26 (top)
Scholnick, Mildred/Marine Mammal Images: 36 (middle)
Schulman, Alisa/Marine Mammal Images: 34 (top)
Slapins, Andris/ Smithsonian Institution: From the exhibition catalogue Crossroads of Continents: Cultures of Siberia and Alaska.: 29
Smithsonian Institution: On loan from the Museum of Anthropology and Ethnography in Leningrad. From the exhibition Crossroads of Continents: Cultures of Siberia and Alaska.: 18, 19 (top right)
Swartz, Steve L.: 30, 59 (left)

Talbot, Bob: 62 (bottom)
Tatoosh Island, Cape Flattery, 1880s/Courtesy of the Seattle Art Museum: 20 (top & middle left)
The Kendall Whaling Museum, Sharon, Massachusetts: 16
Thompson, Art: 20 (bottom right)
Trousset, Leon/Amon Carter Museum, Fort Worth, Texas: 26 (middle)
Washington State Historical Society: 19 (bottom), 20 (middle right)
Webster, Steven K.: 9 (middle)
White, Doc/Ocean Images, Inc.: 4
Wick, Silvan/Marine Mammal Images: 63
Wu, Norbert: 59 (right)
Würsig, Bernd: 12 (middle right), 52-53

Series and Book Editor: Nora L. Deans
Designer: James Stockton, James Stockton & Associates
Printed in Hong Kong through Interprint, Petaluma, California

CONTENTS

Gulls wheel overhead, greeting the dawn with their loud and plaintive cries. Far below, a shoal of silvery fish travels in tight formation through the turbid waters of Mexico's San Ignacio Lagoon. Wading birds forage for food on the strip of sandy beach exposed at low tide.

In the center of the lagoon a massive, barnacle-encrusted mother gray whale drifts in the mild breezes at dawn. Even at this early hour, she keeps a watchful eye on her young calf nearby. A little over three weeks old, the 15-foot, 2,000-pound calf can barely fend for itself in the calm, protected waters of the Mexican lagoon.

As the sun breaks through the morning mists, it reveals many other mothers and calves. Close to a hundred have entered the lagoon in recent weeks, joining another 250 single males and females. The whales have traveled far—farther, in fact, than any other migratory mammal known—to reach their seasonal breeding grounds in these warm waters.

The gray whales of San Ignacio and other Mexican calving lagoons will have barely enough time to rest from their long journey. In a matter of months, they'll leave these lagoons, setting off for distant feeding grounds in cold Arctic seas. Over the course of a year, the whales will journey up and down nearly the full length of the Pacific coast of North America. And every year for the rest of their lives, most gray whales will embark on this incredible migration from warm lagoons to icy seas and back.

1

THE GRAY WHALE

Gray whales (*Eschrichtius robustus*) appear each winter in the lagoons of Baja California, a narrow peninsula along Mexico's Pacific coast. Whales have been coming here for thousands, perhaps hundreds of thousands, of years. The lagoons mark the halfway point of the gray whale's annual migration—an incredible journey that's as much a part of the gray whale as its skin, blubber and bones. It's a migration spanning three seas—the Chukchi, Bering and North Pacific—a journey that's greater than that of any other species of mammal.

Traveling between feeding grounds in Alaska's Bering, Chukchi and Beaufort seas and the breeding lagoons of Baja California, a gray whale may cover about 10,000 miles, and must endure water temperatures ranging from 41 to 72° F. Keeping time with an inner biological clock, the gray whale population moves south along the Pacific coast during the fall and winter (October to early February), returning north during the late winter and spring (mid-February to early June). Seldom during their journeys are grays more than a few miles from shore.

This predictable nearshore migration has brought the gray whale both tragedy and salvation. Pushed by whale hunters to the brink of extinction twice in less than 150 years, gray whales have been seriously over-exploited in the past. Yet the very nearness that put them at risk has also given whale biologists and whale watchers the chance to study these great whales up close.

GRAY WHALES & KIN Gray whales belong to an order of mammals called cetaceans that includes not only whales but also porpoises and dolphins. Like fish, cetaceans live their entire lives in the water. Unlike fish, cetaceans are warm-blooded mammals, with body temperatures that stay more or less stable throughout their lives. Whales breathe air using lungs and give birth to live young which they suckle like other mammals.

Gray whales are one of approximately 80 species of cetaceans living in the world's oceans. Whales and their kin range in length from 4 to 100 feet, and weigh anywhere from 70 to 300,000 pounds. Each species is particularly well adapted to meet the challenges of its marine environment. All cetaceans eat other animals—although only one, the killer whale (*Orcinus orca*), routinely feeds on other warm-blooded prey. The rest thrive on a vast array of cold-blooded foods—everything from tiny shrimplike krill (Euphausiidae) to the 50-foot giant squid (*Architeuthis* sp.) of the deep sea.

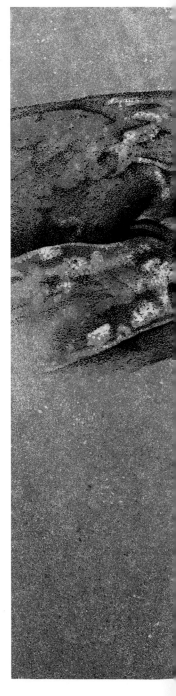

Gray whales travel more than 10,000 miles each year, almost always within a few miles of the coast. While we've learned much about their behavior, grays still remain a mystery in many ways.

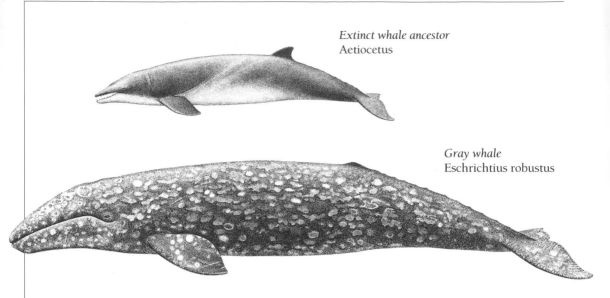

Extinct whale ancestor
Aetiocetus

Gray whale
Eschrichtius robustus

FIFTY MILLION YEARS OF CHANGE The earliest ancestors of whales lived on land about 50 million years ago, although scientists have not yet identified the direct ancestor of modern gray whales. As their descendants gradually adapted to life in the water, a series of physical changes took place. Over many generations, the animals lost nearly all body hair. Their nostrils gradually moved from the tips of their snouts to the tops of their skulls. Forelimbs were transformed into broad, flat paddles. Hindlimbs disappeared. A new feature appeared—a long, muscular tail stock tipped with two horizontal blades we call flukes.

Only a few partial skeletons and one complete skeleton of early gray whales have ever been found, making it difficult to identify their oldest relative. Gray whales continue to pose an evolutionary puzzle. For most of this century scientists have believed that grays were descended from the cetotheres, based on the work of pioneer whale biologists. The Cetotheridae, an extinct family of whales, date back some 38 million years. From other ancient fossil remains we have learned that, at its peak about 15 million years ago, the Cetotheridae family contained more than 50 different species of small and medium-sized whales. A long-held theory proposed that grays, by means of some minor modifications, could have evolved from these cetotheres. Recently, however, that view has been challenged. In the conspicuous absence of any fossil remains linking the earliest modern gray whale, which is a mere 50,000 to 120,000 years old, to the far more ancient cetotheres, some scientists are unwilling to link them to any of the known early whales. So grays have been placed in their own family, Eschrichtidae.

Perhaps, like the walrus, the gray evolved in the north Atlantic and immigrated into the north Pacific during warmer times and higher sea levels. Ultimately, the discovery of new fossils and the use of new technologies that let us study the grays' DNA may help us better understand how gray whales are related to other whales.

All baleen whales alive today, including gray whales, may have evolved indirectly from an extinct family of toothed whales similar to Aetiocetus, pictured above, which lived 25 to 40 million years ago. To date, no fossils of a direct gray whale ancestor have been found.

MODERN WHALES Biologists group living whales into two major categories—toothed whales, the odontocetes, and the baleen whales, or mysticetes. All toothed whales have teeth, as their name implies. Familiar toothed whales include sperm whales (*Physeter macrocephalus*) and close to 70 other species of porpoises, dolphins and beaked whales.

Baleen whales, on the other hand, are toothless. Literally translated, the name *Mysticeti* means "moustached whale." Among the baleen whales are humpbacks (*Megaptera novaeangliae*) and the largest animal that has ever lived on earth—the blue whale (*Balaenoptera musculus*). Early in this century whalers caught and measured adult blue whales more than 100 feet long.

Baleen whales use a thick "moustache" that's really a fringed curtain of baleen to capture and strain shrimplike krill and other small swimming, drifting or burrowing animals from the surrounding sea water or sediments. Several baleen whales feed on small schooling fishes like anchovies and herring.

In place of teeth on the upper jaw, baleen hangs down from the roof of the whale's mouth in a series of horny, overlapping plates. Made of keratin, baleen is the same material as your fingernails. The inner margin of each plate of baleen is fringed with bristles. From afar, the plates look like the teeth of a big, fuzzy comb.

Most baleen whales, like humpbacks, usually "gulp" food from the sea. A feeding whale opens its mouth, takes in a huge mouthful of animal-rich marine soup, then forces this mixture through the baleen. The baleen acts as a natural sieve, trapping small animals inside the whale's mouth but allowing water to pass through. A large whale can extract many pounds of highly nutritious food in a single gulp. The baleen plates of gulper whales are relatively short, and the individual bristles are coarse, allowing the whale to strain and eat small schooling fishes, krill and other tiny animals.

Coarse bristles of baleen hang in rows from a gray whale's upper jaw. As many as 140 to 180 plates fill each side of the gray's mouth.

Some baleen whales, like right whales (*Balaena glacialis*), "skim" the surface. A whale skims by swimming with its mouth open, allowing water to flow in at the front and out at the sides. Food gets trapped on the inner surface of the baleen and is pushed back by the whale's tongue or gets washed down with a gush of sea water into the throat. The baleen plates of these whales can be incredibly long, up to 12 feet, and are fringed with fine, hairlike bristles. A skimming whale strains its way through huge swarms of krill and even smaller·sea creatures.

Gray whales, under normal circumstances, are neither gulpers nor skimmers. Rather, they have developed a feeding strategy all their own, and could best be called "suckers." They work the shallows of northern seas, creating rectangular pits as they suck up sand and mud from the bottom and force it out through their baleen. Small animals that live buried in the mud get trapped on the baleen plates, which are quite short and stiff and have extremely coarse bristles. This kind of baleen is well-suited for separating the whales' preferred food—tiny amphipods—from the muddy sediment.

Grays will only rarely act like gulpers. Should the opportunity present itself, a gray whale might gulp anchovies, smelt or other small schooling creatures swimming by. But by and large, the gray whale is a bottom feeder, a diner on the protein-rich muck of Arctic seafloors.

SHADES OF GRAY   Some scientists think that gray whales may be the most "primitive" living baleen whales, having changed relatively little over millions of years. Evidence for this view might include their slow swimming speeds and the resulting heavy fouling by barnacles, their preference for nearshore waters and bottom feeding, and their dependence on sheltered lagoons for calving. These behaviors contrast sharply with the swifter open-ocean feeders and breeders like fin whales and blue whales. Other characteristics of a less-evolved species could include the gray's coarse baleen, a virtual lack of throat pleats that allow the mouth to engulf large quantities of food, and the absence of a well-developed dorsal fin—grays only have a small dorsal hump. Some scientists, however, don't believe these are "primitive" characteristics at all. They consider these to be secondarily derived characteristics that evolved later to meet what they say are the specialized, highly evolved needs of grays. Both views continue to underscore the puzzle that gray whales pose to biologists.

In the wild, an adult gray whale is impressive to behold. A 45-foot, 35-ton gray is roughly the same size and weight as 10 good-sized elephants. Its broad back, which lacks a dorsal fin but possesses a series of knuckle-like ridges or bumps, distinguishes the gray whale from any other species of whale.

A gray whale's triangular, bowed head takes up roughly one-sixth of its total body length. Seen up close, the face of a gray whale is curiously craggy. Thick, widely spaced bristles sprout from the top of its head and along its lower jaw. These bristles and their pit-like follicles are especially noticeable on newborn gray whales.

Grooves on a whale's throat allow it to expand when feeding. Grays only have two to four grooves, fewer than other baleen whales.

Eight feet from the tip of the jaw are the whale's eyes. Each eye, about the size of a baseball, is placed so far back on its head that true stereoscopic vision as we know it is impossible. To get a good look at an object on either side of it, the gray whale must move its entire body. However, gray whales do seem to have limited stereoscopic vision directed downward, which would help them in looking at their feeding grounds on the seafloor.

On the top of the gray's head, directly above its eyes, is a pair of blowholes that are, in fact, nostrils. Because its blowholes are so high up on its head, a gray can breathe by barely breaking the surface of the water. The blowholes connect directly to the lungs, so breathing doesn't interfere with anything else. A swimming gray whale's mouth may be full of water, but it won't miss a breath.

A gray whale sports 6 to 12 knobs on its back (top left) and raised twin blowholes (top right). Its eyes (above) see both in dimly lit waters and in the air.

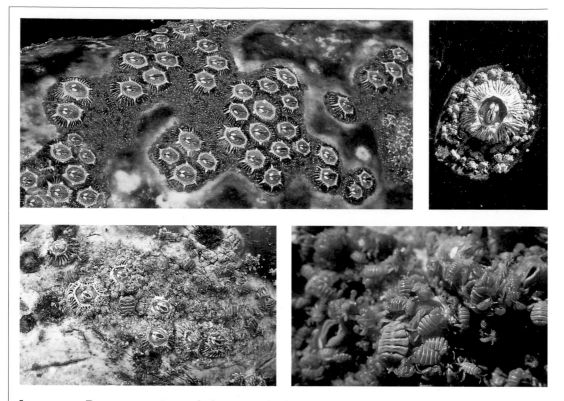

LADEN WITH PARASITES   Gray whales carry the heaviest parasite load of all cetaceans. Thousands of small hitchhiking invertebrates live firmly attached to the whale's head and body.

Whitish blotches on the skin of each whale may be dense clusters of a barnacle, *Cryptolepas rhachianecti*, that attach exclusively to gray whales. Once they have settled on "their" gray, these small crustaceans spend their entire lives in the same place. Other barnacles may settle on rocks or floating objects, like logs or debris.

The whale barnacles, snug in their hard limestone shells, stick out feathery feet to comb the sea, capturing plankton and other minute food. As larvae, the barnacles are free-swimming, but soon they attach themselves to the skin of newborn calves in the lagoons. This barnacle species seems to time its reproductive activities so that the free-swimming larvae are ready to settle out on the newly arriving grays and their newborns. For these hangers-on, life aboard a gray whale is good: as the young gray whales grow, so do the barnacle clusters, eventually forming large, solid white colonies, especially on the whale's head, flippers, back and tail flukes.

Stories abound about gray whales rubbing against rocks to rid themselves of barnacles. But there is no reliable evidence of this occurring in U.S. waters. Observers in the Soviet Union, however, report that grays in Siberian waters rub themselves along some pebble beaches. These whales also enter brackish lagoons and, briefly, the mouths of rivers. At both of these locations, the whales leave behind quantities of shed barnacles.

Another type of hitchhiker clings to the gray whale's throat grooves, skin folds, blowholes and barnacle clusters. Called whale

Heavy clusters of barnacles surrounded by whale lice adorn gray whales (top left). Barnacles (top right) are just along for the ride and don't harm the whales.

Whale lice, however, like those above, actually feed on the whale.

lice, but not really lice at all, these animals are amphipods, more closely related to the bottom-dwelling amphipods that gray whales eat. Three different species of whale lice are found on gray whales. Two species, *Cyamus scammoni* and *Cyamus kessleri*, are found on no other kind of whale, while the third, *Cyamus ceti*, commonly hitchhikes on other cetaceans.

Whale lice, unlike barnacles, are true parasites that feed on gray whale skin and damaged tissue. They tend to gather around open wounds or scars. Whale lice may transfer from mother whales to their calves during birth, nursing and other day-to-day bodily contact. The largest of the three whale louse species, *C. scammoni*, is also the most abundant. One hundred thousand of these parasites have been found on a single gray whale.

Skin care for gray whales comes in part in the form of topsmelt (*Atherinops affinis*), silvery fish that school in San Ignacio and other breeding lagoons. Ordinarily, topsmelt feed on marine plants, tiny shrimps and other minute creatures of the lagoons. But when the whales are around, topsmelt supplement their diets in a rather ingenious way. Schools of these small fish pick at the barnacles and whale lice encrusting a gray whale's skin. A closer look reveals that topsmelt are not only feeding on these parasites but also on flakes from the outermost layer of the gray's skin. For topsmelt, the flakes are an abundant source of protein-rich food.

Topsmelt cleaners may benefit the whales, too. By ridding them of some of their parasites and old, flaky skin, topsmelt may be decreasing the resistance, or drag, that grays create as their huge bodies move through the water.

Whale biologists tell individual grays apart by their patterns of barnacle clusters—no two are alike. Because barnacles orient into the current, their distribution on a whale indicates water flow around and over the whale.

Topsmelt groom whales in the calving lagoons.

A WHALE OF MANY NAMES

Known in Japan as 'the small whale,' a 50-foot adult gray is dwarfed by larger species of whales.

The gray whale gets its modern common name from its dull, mottled, charcoal-gray skin. Yet throughout history, this great whale has been called by many other names.

Some of the oldest sightings of what may have been gray whales found their way into the manuscripts and published reports of English and Icelandic explorers of the north Atlantic Ocean. As far back as the early seventeenth century, rather cryptic reports refer to a whale called the "otta sotta" or "sandloegja." An Icelandic manuscript contains the earliest known illustration of a gray.

The earliest scientific reference to the gray whale was made by an English naturalist, the Honorable Paul Dudley, in an essay published in 1725 by the Royal Society of London. "The Scrag Whale," observed Dudley, "is near of kin to the Fin-back, but instead of a Fin upon his Back, the Ridge of the Afterpart of his Back is scragged with half a Dozen Knobs; he is nearest the right Whale in Figure and for Quantity of Oil; his bone is white but will not split."

Dudley's "scrag" was just one of several names New England whalers used to describe their quarry. Pacific coast whalers called this same animal the "hard head," "mussel digger," "devilfish" and "rip-sack" whale. Across the Pacific, in Japan, the gray whale was known as "Kokujira," the small whale.

In 1777, a prominent German veterinarian, J. P. Erxleben gave the gray whale the scientific name, *Balaena gibbosa*—literally "humped whale" in Latin. The name stuck; whale scientists used it for nearly 200 years. Later, *Balaena gibbosa* became *Rhachianectes glaucus*, "the gray swimmer along rocky shores." This name was soon replaced with the gray's current scientific name, *Eschrichtius robustus*, a name given in 1864 to honor Danish zoologist Daniel Eschricht.

Its knobby back earned the gray whale one of its many nicknames.

THE INSIDE STORY   Beneath the supple, parasite-encrusted skin of the gray whale lies a six-inch layer of blubber. It may serve primarily as an energy reserve, sustaining the whale during trips to and from the Arctic feeding grounds. The all-encompassing jacket of fat ensures that the gray will stay warm even in the coldest of seas.

The insulating influence of blubber is aided by a specially adapted circulatory system. The gray's arteries and veins run side by side underneath its skin in tight bundles, enabling cooled blood from the surface to be warmed before it returns to the heart.

The whale's heart and other internal organs are surrounded by muscle and bone. Despite the differences in size and the modifications over time, it's still possible to find a human equivalent for virtually every bone in the gray whale's body.

WHALE INTELLIGENCE   How intelligent are whales? There is a common and widespread assumption that all cetaceans are extremely intelligent. Their large and complex brains, and the ease with which some dolphins learn "tricks," seem to indicate a high order of intelligence. Yet defining intelligence is incredibly difficult. Attempts to determine human intelligence are often controversial, and it becomes an even more complex task to study the intelligence of an animal with whom we cannot communicate. So far, there is no overwhelming evidence that cetaceans are more intelligent than any other highly evolved social mammal.

In arguments about intelligence, biologists often consider brain size or the weight of the brain as a percent of body weight. When you compare the ratio of brain volume to body surface area among cetaceans, there is great variety among species. The ratio is lowest in river dolphins and largest in bottlenose dolphins which are highly social, live in groups and care for their slowly maturing young for long periods.

Brain complexity also enters into arguments about intelligence. In cetaceans, while the folding patterns are complex, they more closely resemble the folding patterns in the brains of mammals like cattle and deer rather than exhibiting the complexity of human brains.

Grays, and other baleen whales, do not have disproportionately large brains. However, their brains are particularly well developed in those regions responsible for processing sounds from their environment. Also, grays and other baleen whales are not currently known to form lasting bonds with closely related individuals, unlike highly social bottlenose dolphins and killer whales. It's interesting to note, however, that the very low frequency sounds of some baleen whales can be heard for miles, even for hundreds of miles. Staying in touch and being "social" may take on a different meaning for gray whales.

While gray whales may not be considered highly social, they do exhibit caregiving, as do many other cetaceans. Siberian whalers report that grays will attend, support or remain with a wounded whale. In the breeding lagoons, live-stranded calves have been pushed back into tidal channels by the mother and an unrelated adult in apparent acts of reciprocal assistance.

Most of what little we do know about baleen whale intelligence is inferred, and our understanding may remain limited in light of the difficulties in carrying out experiments with these huge, free-ranging animals. Questions of animal awareness or "sense of self" intrigue biologists, psychologists and philosophers alike. Our understanding slowly grows as each group develops fresh experiments and discusses its findings.

THE RANGE OF GRAY WHALES Gray whales now live only in the Pacific Ocean, but they were once more widespread than they are today. By reviewing whalers' records and reports, and by studying skeletons and other ancient remains of whales, we've pieced together a more global picture of gray whale populations.

Complete and partial gray whale skeletons that are subfossils (calcified but not yet mineralized) have been found from both Europe and the east coast of North America. They reveal that gray whales once lived on both sides of the Atlantic Ocean. The oldest North American specimens—pieces of a juvenile whale's skull recovered near the mouth of Chesapeake Bay in Virginia—are around 10,000 years old. The most recent North American specimen—a jawbone from Southampton, New York—belonged to a whale that lived during early colonial times. From these few finds, however, we can only guess at the numbers of whales that once swam in the north Atlantic Ocean. And while we don't know the cause of their demise, it curiously coincides with the development of whaling in both Europe and America.

Gray whales once inhabited Korean waters in fair numbers, but the current status of these animals remains in serious doubt. As many as 40 have been seen in recent years near the island of Sakhalin in Russian waters off northern Japan. Gray whales may have been found in the Sea of Japan and along the Pacific coasts of several Japanese islands prior to the 1900s, according to old books about whaling, whaling reports dating back to the 1600s,

A stylized baleen whale may have represented a gray whale on a 1798 Japanese watercolor scroll, Twenty-three Varieties of Whales.

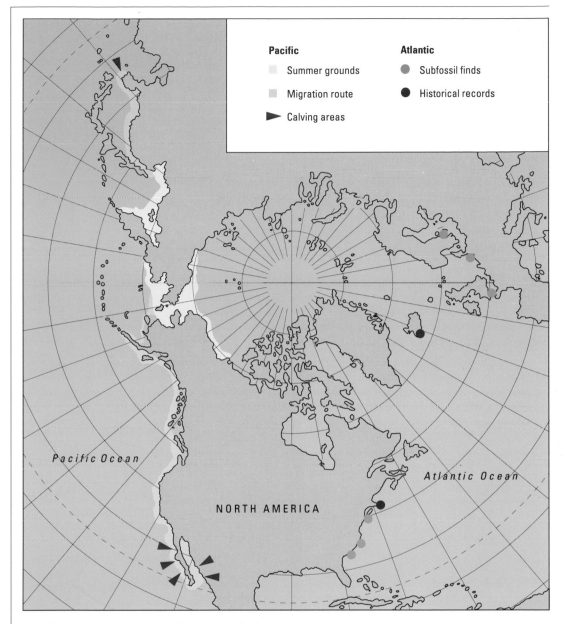

Pacific
- Summer grounds
- Migration route
- ► Calving areas

Atlantic
- Subfossil finds
- Historical records

Pacific Ocean

Atlantic Ocean

NORTH AMERICA

and the discovery of several ancient whale jawbones. These animals may have migrated along the east coast of Korea, reaching Japanese waters in winter. Korean whalers captured about 1,500 animals from 1910 to 1933, giving up the hunt only after they ran out of whales.

By the mid-1870s, intensive commercial whaling by ship and from shore stations had reduced the population of whales along the Pacific coast of North America to about 4,000 animals. Protected from further exploitation by international treaty in 1946 and by the Marine Mammal Protection Act of 1972, this population swiftly rebounded. Approximately 21,000 gray whales now live in the eastern Pacific Ocean, very possibly as many as existed before the heyday of commercial whaling.

Gray whales once ranged more widely than they do today. The Korean population is nearly extinct, but new evidence suggests grays occurred recently and historically on the southeast coast of China.

2

HAUNTED BY HUNTERS

The gray whale's predictable nearshore migration route and its highly visible spout made it an easy target for the first whalers of the Pacific coast. Evidence uncovered by archaeologists in the Aleutian Islands of Alaska, along the coast of British Columbia and in Washington state points to a handful of whaling cultures that existed for thousands of years before the arrival of the first European whalers. Two Northwest Coast groups were especially skilled at hunting gray whales and other cetaceans: the Nuchanult, formerly known as the Nootka, a vast nation of Native American tribes who lived on Canada's Vancouver Island, and the Makah tribe of Washington's Olympic Peninsula.

Using wooden harpoons tipped with mussel shell blades, lines made out of braided whale sinew and inflated floats made of sealskin, eight-man crews of Makah tribesmen routinely launched their 30-foot dugout canoes in search of gray whales. The Makah called their quarry *sih-wah-wihw,* the "beings with itchy faces"—a name inspired by the gray's gnarly, barnacle-clad head.

After a whale was captured and brought ashore, it was cut up and distributed with much ceremony and ritual. The actual business of cutting up the animal was supervised by the harpooner. Special portions were given to the crew and the remainder went to members of the tribe.

The imposing shapes of five whales are carved deep into the rock at Cape Alava, immediately south of the modern-day Makah reservation. These rock carvings, surrounded by many small, oval-shaped fertility symbols, serve as reminders of the importance the Makahs placed on whaling. As recently as 1913, Makahs continued to hunt for whales using traditional methods.

Researchers disagree about which whales the Nuchanult hunted off the coast of Vancouver Island. Some say gray whales were most frequently caught; others believe that the Nuchanult focused their efforts on humpbacks. This latter theory is backed by evidence from ancient Native American refuse heaps, called middens, on the west coast of Vancouver Island. The shells of barnacles that live on humpback whales are more commonly unearthed at these archeological sites.

Nuchanult hunters used methods very similar to those of the Makah. However, the ceremonies surrounding the kill and butchering of whales varied from one tribal group to the next. One family, for example, customarily sacrificed a slave in honor of the first whale killed in a season.

Lacking wood, Asian Eskimos and other northern cultures made household implements, like this whalebone bucket, from parts of whales.

Edward S. Curtis photographed this Makah whaler (below) holding a harpoon attached to sealskin floats. The floats prevented the whale from diving once harpooned.

The flat wooden objects (right) may be Aleutian dance mask attachments depicting, among other things, a harpoon.

Makah whalers hunted grays and other whales, including humpbacks (bottom left), from their large ocean-going cedar canoes.

Farther north in Alaska and Siberia, early whale hunters dipped their harpoon tips in aconite, a strong poison made from the root of the monkshood plant (*Aconitum napellus*). After striking a whale, they waited for the aconite to take effect and for their quarry to float at the surface. Whale hunting continues to be practiced by the Inuit of Alaska and Canada, the natives of the Siberian coast and by several other aboriginal cultures today.

While we doubt that the natives of Baja California ever hunted gray whales, drawings on the walls of caves just north of Magdalena Lagoon show that the first residents knew about whales and whale hunting. One cave drawing shows a whale with a number of harpoons sticking out of it. Another depicts a well-defined porpoise and her baby. No firm dates have been established for these and other examples of cave art in Baja California, but most are believed to be at least 500 to 1,000 years old.

Northwest Coast art depicts a baleen whale.

CHARLES MELVILLE SCAMMON 1825-1911

Although Charles Scammon was born in Pittston, Maine on May 28, 1825, he was not to remain in New England for long. By age 25, Scammon was firmly ensconced aboard a schooner cruising the largely unexplored California coast. Two years later, he took command of the brig *Mary Helen*, sailing to Mexico in search of seals, sea lions and whales. During the Civil War he commanded a revenue cutter in San Francisco; in 1865 he plied Siberian and Alaskan waters; between 1868 and 1870 he explored the Strait of Juan de Fuca in Washington state; and by 1880 he was stationed in Florida, the commander of a side-wheel steamer, the *John A. Dix*. In 1895 Scammon, the distinguished seaman, retired from active service.

During Scammon's extensive travels, he observed a vast array of animals, everything from the sea otters and whales in cold northern seas to the manatees in Florida's warm channels and springs. A self-taught naturalist, he eagerly described, measured and sketched the living objects of his interest. Assisted by renowned naturalists Edward Drinker Cope, curator of the Philadelphia Academy of Sciences at the time, and William Healey Dall of the Smithsonian Institution, Scammon put his observations of marine mammals into

Scammon posed in his dress uniform in 1866.

print. For several decades after its release in 1874, his book, *The Marine Mammals of the Northwestern Coast of North America*, was thought to contain the most comprehensive portrait available of the gray whale.

Whaling ships in San Francisco, Scammon's home port during his heyday as a whaling captain.

HUNTED AGAIN The impact of aboriginal whaling on gray whale stocks was slight, especially compared to the wholesale slaughter of gray whales by the first European whalers on the Pacific coast. The first non-native Americans to capture gray whales were called "shore whalers." Shore whaling, as defined by early naturalist and whaling captain Charles Melville Scammon, involved pursuing whales from a small boat launched from shore.

Shore whaling was hard work: the hunters' 28-foot boats were powered simply by sail or by oar, and the six crew members might have to row for hours to chase down a whale. Because they used hand-thrown harpoons, crew members had to get very close and throw their harpoons with great force. The whale might tow them for hours before it tired. The exhausted whale was killed using knives on long poles or exploding bomb-lances. After all this, the whalers still had to tow their 35-ton catch back to shore.

The first shore whaling station appeared on the California coast in 1854. The Monterey Whaling Company was owned and managed by Captain J.P. Davenport, a transplanted whaler from Rhode Island. Davenport's contribution to central California life is remembered today in the small town north of Santa Cruz that bears his name.

During Davenport's time, whale oil, not whale meat or baleen, was the sought-after prize. Whale blubber was stripped from the carcasses on shore through a process called "flensing." The blubber was then minced and tossed into huge vats, heated and rendered into oil. The oil from gray whales was considered inferior to the oil of other whales. Still, oil production was a lucrative venture, considering that each whale carcass yielded between 25 and 45 barrels of oil, and, in those days, the market price for a barrel ranged from $27 to $45.

It wasn't long before the Monterey area became the hub of shore whaling activity. As the success of these stations became known,

Crews in small whale boats set out from whaling ships to pursue grays along California's coast.

613 — FIRST BRICK HOUSE IN CALIFORNIA AND OLD WHALING STATION.

other stations set up operation. Shore whaling stations soon appeared along the length of the California coast, from Crescent City in the north to San Diego in the south. Many of these stations were manned by Portuguese whalers, hard-working and frugal opportunists who left their settlements in the Azore and Cape Verde Islands to make a living in America.

The Portuguese Whaling Company, Monterey's second shore whaling company, opened its doors in 1855. Each year for the next three years, this Portuguese-owned business processed about 800 barrels of oil, mainly from humpback whales.

Most of California's shore whaling stations were small-scale operations, staffed largely by people who spent the bulk of the year working on farms when not whaling. The sudden proliferation of shore whaling stations alone could have put severe pressure on the gray whale, but it was the discovery of the breeding lagoons in Baja California that really opened the door for the wholesale slaughter of gray whales.

Credit for discovering the gray whale's breeding grounds in the eastern Pacific Ocean goes to Charles Scammon, captain of the American whaling ship *Boston*. In 1855, the *Boston* sailed from San Francisco bound for Mexico on a seal and whale hunting mission. "The objects of our pursuit were found in great numbers," Scammon wrote of this particular voyage, "and the opportunities for studying their habits were so good that I became greatly interested in collecting facts bearing upon the natural history of these animals."

It was on this journey that Scammon and his crew happened upon the shallow Laguna Ojo de Liebre or "Jackrabbit Spring

The Old Whaling Station in Monterey, photographed in 1902 housed Portuguese whalers working for Captain J. Davenport. The restored house is now part of the state's Monterey Historic Park.

Lagoon," later renamed Scammon's Lagoon. Here, and in two other lagoons on the peninsula, he found an unexpected abundance of gray whale mothers and calves—whales that were easy to reach from the whalers' established ports in San Francisco and Hawaii. As word of Scammon's find rapidly spread, whaling ships were dispatched to hunt the gray whales in the lagoons. Guerrero Negro Lagoon was named after one of these vessels, the bark *Black Warrior* from Honolulu. *Black Warrior* was caught by fierce winds, smashed against the shore and wrecked as it was being towed out of the lagoon in 1858.

This well-known frontispiece from Scammon's classic whaling account depicts lagoons in Baja California full of gray whales and ships.

Schooners, with shallow drafts capable of negotiating the twisting channels and treacherous sandbars in the lagoons, were the most efficient whaling vessels. Ships with deeper hulls anchored outside the lagoons, sending in smaller whaleboats to hunt the whales in the otherwise inaccessible reaches of the lagoons. Still other ships simply waited at anchor, ambushing the grays as they swam out of the lagoons.

Once inside the lagoons, whalers from large and small ships slaughtered any whale within reach of their harpoons. Like virtually all other whalers, they showed neither mercy nor thought for the continued existence of the gray whale. Tragically, the animals most likely to be encountered in the lagoons were either pregnant cows or mothers and calves. All of these whales were exceptionally easy to chase down and kill. Accelerating the demise of the grays, whalers frequently used Greener's harpoon gun, a swivel-mounted weapon that made hunting for large whales from small boats even less of a risk. The gun, as described by Scammon, was able to shoot a four-and-a-half-foot harpoon "with considerable accuracy to any distance under 80 yards."

Scammon, fifth from the right, posed with his wife (far right) and crew on the deck of a revenue cutter in the 1860s.

After only four years of intensive whaling, Scammon's Lagoon was essentially emptied of whales. By 1874, the same year that Scammon published his authoritative book, *The Marine Mammals of the Northwestern Coast of North America, Together with an account of the American Whale-Fishery*, an estimated 10,000 to 11,300 gray whales were killed by whalers working the Pacific coast. Scammon wrote:

" . . . the large bays and lagoons, where the animals once congregated, brought forth and nurtured their young, are already nearly deserted. The mammoth bones of the California Gray Whale lie bleaching on the shores of those silvery waters, and are scattered along the broken coasts, from Siberia to the Gulf of California; and ere long it may be questioned whether this mammal will not be numbered among the extinct species of the Pacific."

The North American population of gray whales had suffered a massive blow. Extinction loomed on the horizon.

THE HUNT ABANDONED It hadn't taken long for this new crop of whalers to reduce the eastern Pacific's gray whale population to a fraction of its former abundance. By 1880, so few whales had survived this onslaught that hunting the gray was no longer profitable either for shore whalers or whalers from ships. Inexpensive kerosene had been introduced, further depressing the market for whale oil. The last whale ever to be taken by California's shore whalers was a humpback, towed into Monterey Bay in 1905. This massive reduction in the gray whale population caused extensive starvation among those Siberian native whalers who depended upon the summer appearance of grays in their coastal waters.

California shore whalers stripped blubber from grays in the shallows.

Fourteen years later, a new type of whaling station started to operate from Moss Landing in Monterey Bay. Built by Pacific Coast Sea Products, this station used a pair of steam-powered catcher boats to hunt the whales, primarily humpbacks. The bodies were inflated with air to keep them from sinking, then towed ashore. At the station, modern steam-driven winches, slicers and cookers processed each whale in less than an hour. The meat was ground into fertilizer, the bones into bone meal. Blubber chunks were sliced and rendered into oil, then sold to a company that made soap. The station remained in business until 1925, taking over 700 humpbacks and depleting the local population.

Humpback whale bones (top) await processing at Pacific Coast Sea Products Whaling Station at Moss Landing around 1919.

Whale bones litter the beach in a painting of Monterey in 1875 by Leon Trousset (above).

AN ADVENTURER'S SEARCH FOR GRAYS In 1912, zoologist Roy Chapman Andrews "rediscovered" the gray whale, believed extinct in American waters. Four years earlier, while visiting Japan, Andrews learned of a whale called "Kokujira," the target of whalers in Korea. Kokujira's description so closely matched that of the gray that Andrews' curiosity led him to a whaling station in Ulsan, Korea. No sooner had he boarded a boat at Ulsan than the zoologist's suspicions were confirmed.

Andrews' findings were presented in a monograph on the gray whale in Korea, published by the American Museum of Natural History in 1914. In *Whale Hunting With Gun and Camera*, Andrews later shared his experiences in Korean seas with an audience of non-scientists:

"We had hardly left the shore, when the siren whistle of a whale ship sounded far down the bay and soon the vessel swept around the point into view. At the port bow hung the dark flukes of a whale, the sight of which made me breathe hard with excitement, for one of two things must happen—either I was to find that there was an entirely new species or else was to rediscover one which had been lost to science for 30 years."

Andrews' jubilation was short-lived. Faced with the same pressures from whale hunters as their American cousins, the Korean population of gray whales was also destined to decline.

In 1912, Roy Chapman Andrews watched as Japanese whalers at Ulsan, Korea cut into a gray whale, believed extinct in the region. Two Korean observers in traditional long, white coats, baggy trousers and horsehair hats stand in the foreground.

THE HUNT RESUMED The whalers' economically inspired cease-fire gave gray whales the opportunity to stage a comeback. Somehow, perhaps by finding new, less-accessible breeding grounds further south along the Mexican mainland, grays began to multiply again. Population growth remained unchecked until 1914, the year that the first of several Norwegian factory ships appeared off Magdalena Bay. Any whales left alive after the hunt of the mid- to late-1800s were fair game for the chaser boats that supplied these floating factories with whales. The chasers were equipped with a broad arsenal of modern weapons including exploding harpoons, deadly contraptions invented in Norway 50 years earlier.

The large floating whale processors were fast and efficient. Aboard ship, nothing was wasted but the whale. Whales were lifted out of the water using hydraulic hoists, then flensed by machine and boiled down in huge blubber pots on deck. According to the catch records of these floating factories, 181 gray whales were processed between December, 1924 and March, 1929.

The Norwegians were joined by the whale ships of Soviet, Japanese and American interests. Numbers of whales plummeted for a second time in less than a century. Whaling continued into the 1940s, even after an international agreement ostensibly put an end to the killing in 1937.

In 1946, measures to fully protect the now-endangered gray whale were implemented. The International Convention for the Regulation of Whaling became the second treaty signed by the various whaling nations. However, by this time there were few whales to protect. And even after the agreement went into effect, some nations continued to hunt grays. The Soviet Union, for example, exercised its right to take grays, citing a special provision that allows governments to kill whales to feed Eskimos or other aboriginal people whose traditional needs include whale flesh. The Soviet hunt continues to this day, taking 179 whales each year to feed aboriginal residents of coastal Siberia. In recent decades, these whales have been used for an unsanctioned purpose—to feed foxes at Soviet-owned fur farms near the Siberian whaling villages.

While a small number of gray whales are still legally hunted, years of protection from commercial whaling have allowed gray whale populations to grow to over 21,000.

In 1972, the United States Congress passed the Marine Mammal Protection Act, which set a moratorium on the taking of any marine mammals by Americans and on the importation of marine mammals or marine mammal products. Primary responsibility for the protection of gray whales and other marine mammals was given to the U.S. Department of Commerce's National Marine Fisheries Service. A year later, the federal Endangered Species Act gave gray whales and other over-exploited cetaceans further protection. These two important pieces of legislation guaranteed gray whales humane treatment in American seas.

A small number of grays are still taken each summer by Inuit whalers in Alaska. The Inuit prefer to hunt the larger, more docile bowhead whale (*Balaena mysticetus*) over the gray. They consider grays more dangerous when hunted in small boats.

Efforts to safeguard gray whales in North America have been so successful that whale biologists are now asking whether gray whales should continue to be protected under the Endangered Species Act. Under the terms of an 1978 amendment to the act, the status of any endangered animal must be reviewed by a panel of scientists every five years. The conclusions of the panel are first published as a preliminary decision, which is sent out for public review. If the public responds with sufficient rebuttal, the decision is re-examined by the National Marine Fisheries Service and a new, revised conclusion is put forth.

The gray whale retained its endangered status in 1984, having withstood one review. However, with the steady growth of gray whale populations, it is possible that the second review could mark the first time in the history of the Endangered Species Act that any marine mammal has been "de-listed." Protection could be retained under the terms of the Marine Mammal Protection Act.

Siberian children watch as a gray is butchered on the beach on the Chukotka Peninsula The International Whaling Commission allows limited aboriginal or subsistence whaling, which does not endanger grays.

3

LIFE IN MEXICAN LAGOONS

Why do gray whales and certain other mammals, fishes, birds, reptiles and insects migrate to different areas to feed and breed? Migration lets them sample the best of two worlds—the seasonal abundance of food found in colder regions and the nurturing climate for giving birth and rearing young found in warmer regions. It's these seasonal changes that cause most baleen whales to migrate great distances, splitting the year between icy feeding grounds and warm breeding grounds. And while other species do migrate, no other baleen whale or toothed whale habitually travels as far as the gray. Grays may actually save energy by leaving their cold feeding grounds when their food becomes unavailable.

The urge to migrate is very strong in gray whales. We don't know for certain which factors trigger whales to move out, but they may include fewer hours of daylight, changes in water temperature, changes in availability of food as the northern pack ice increases, or changing hormone levels involved in breeding.

Whatever the triggers, gray whales leave their feeding grounds in late summer and begin the journey south. For eligible whales, the breeding season has begun.

GRAY WHALE COURTSHIP Bulls and cows may begin courtship and mating as they head south from the Bering Sea and swim along the Pacific coast toward their southern breeding lagoons. There has been very little research into the social organization of gray whales, unlike the long-term studies of humpback whales, killer whales and bottlenose dolphins. However, from many observations of gray whale courtship and mating activity, biologists think that grays are promiscuous. Both sexes appear to copulate with several partners over the course of the breeding season.

A female gray whale may mate with several males during courting episodes that last two hours or more (left). High-speed chases and lots of splashing are common.

A mother and calf (right) swim in the sheltered waters of a lagoon.

Cows and bulls reach sexual maturity anywhere from five to eleven years of age. They breed during a three-week period, primarily in late November or early December. A few grays may breed as late as the end of January. Cows that give birth in January will usually mate the following year. A few cows will "rest" for a third year, so at any one time, less than half of the sexually mature cows are available to mate. The rest are already carrying or caring for calves.

Because there are twice as many eligible bulls as available cows, the bulls must compete for females. While some pushing and shoving may take place, biologists don't think that full-scale battles over cows occur, as they do among humpbacks and other species of large whales. Two courting bulls often follow the same cow, forming tightly knit trios that remain intact right up to the moment of conception.

Courtship ends when a swimming cow slows down, signaling her willingness to mate. The two bulls move in close, using their flippers to try to slow the cow even more. Eventually, the cow rolls onto her back and the bulls, swimming upside down, approach the cow on either side. Each bull tries to press the advantage, maneuvering ever closer and caressing the cow with his flippers. Finally, copulation occurs when the cow and one of the bulls roll together.

Because females mate with more than one male, and because males don't aggressively fight, biologists suspect that "sperm competition" may be taking place in gray whale fertilization. Bulls have very large testes that produce large amounts of sperm. This strategy appears to rely on overwhelming the competing whales' sperm by sheer quantity, rather than by using exclusive access to the female to achieve fertilization.

THE CALVING LAGOONS Traveling in groups or alone, gray whales may reach San Ignacio and other Mexican breeding lagoons as early as mid-December. Expectant females arrive first. The calves they are carrying were conceived a full year before. The gestation period of a gray whale is nearly 13 months, so even before they're born, calves have already completed the long, round-trip journey along the coast.

The pregnant cows appear to head for the lagoons when the time comes to give birth, although many calves are born during the migration from central California southward. Biologists believe that at least some of the mothers-to-be return to the same lagoons year after year. By January, all of the calving lagoons are filled with whales. The first lagoon births of each season may occur in Guerrero Negro Lagoon, northernmost of the Baja California breeding grounds. Next is Scammon's Lagoon, where each year, according to the National Marine Fisheries Service, more than half of all gray whale calves are born. Recognizing the importance of Guerrero Negro and Scammon's lagoons, the Mexican government protects both of these vital breeding grounds as sanctuaries. They restrict the activities of fishermen, whale watchers and other human intruders when the whales are in the lagoons.

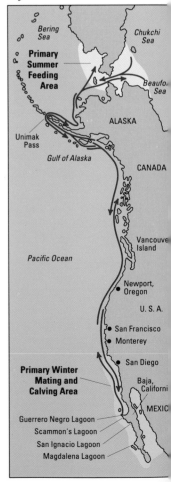

Each year, grays journey from icy feeding grounds to warm breeding lagoons and back, traveling farther than any other mammal.

Farther south along the arid peninsula is San Ignacio Lagoon, also a refuge where access is limited to visitors with government authorization. San Ignacio is also very large, about 4 miles wide by 20 miles long, and is the destination of most chartered whale watching trips. However, between December 15th and March 15th, all commercial boat traffic is confined to the lower third of the lagoon.

Even further south is Magdalena Bay. Less than six percent of all gray whale calves are born here every year. As gray whale populations continue to increase, more whales are seen in the vicinity of Cabo San Lucas at the very tip of the Baja peninsula and, in recent years, pods have been seen as far north in the Sea of Cortez as Bahia de los Angeles.

Of all the large whales, only gray whales seek out warm, shallow lagoons to have their young.

CARING FOR CALVES Soon after they arrive at the lagoons, pregnant cows give birth to single calves. Most births occur between January 5 and February 15—with a peak in births around January 27.

Few people have ever seen a gray whale giving birth, making some whale biologists suspect that the whales give birth at the mouths of the lagoons, then escort their young into the lagoons' sheltered waters. Published accounts of gray whale births cite head-first deliveries, contrary to eyewitness reports of births of dolphins and other toothed whales at marine parks and public aquariums. The majority of these toothed whales births are breech, or tail-first, deliveries.

While pregnant humpback whales in Hawaii are often accompanied by a sexually active escort male, there's no evidence that grays form such relationships. Mother grays, it appears, give birth to their calves alone in shallow water, unattended by others.

Newborn gray whales are large, around 15 feet long, and weigh close to 2,000 pounds. Calves are practically helpless at birth. Their flukes are weak and curled from having been folded inside the mother's womb for many months. A mother supports her calf at the surface for its first few breaths of air, buoying it up with her own back and flukes. Instinct guides the youngster to breathe. While the calf's first swimming movements are uncoordinated, within three hours it keeps itself afloat and swims on a steady course.

Instinct also guides the newborn calf to drink milk from its mother's nipples. These are recessed in shallow slits on the cow's belly, located on either side of the genital opening. When the calf's mouth touches one of the paired folds of skin, muscles push the nipple outward. A stream of thick milk is forcibly directed into the calf's eager mouth.

Rich, nutritious gray whale milk is roughly 50 percent fat, about 15 times the percentage of fat found in cow's milk. Calves drink around 50 gallons of this fat-laden fluid each day, and grow rapidly. By August, when most calves are weaned, the eight-month-old gray whales will have nearly doubled in weight. Calves continue to feed heavily and grow rapidly throughout their first year of life.

A cow's relationship with her calf is especially close, even tender by human terms. A cow will frequently draw her offspring alongside, gently stroking it with her massive flippers, and will let her baby ride on her back for the first few days. Even as a calf grows and begins to show its independence, it remains in close contact, if for no other reason than to nurse or be drawn through the water in the wake of its full-bodied mother. Growing calves may strengthen their abilities to move through the water by swimming treadmill-fashion in the strong tidal currents at the lagoon entrances.

Mothers and calves usually keep to themselves in the inner stretches of the lagoon, staying away from the males and single females. Extremely protective of their young, cows may at times become belligerent when they perceive a threat—real or imagined. Whale hunters were the first people to feel the full force of a mother gray's wrath. Whenever a calf was injured, observed Charles Scammon, captain of the whaling ship *Boston*, "the parent animal, in her frenzy, will chase the boats, and, overtaking them, will overturn them with her head or dash them to pieces with a stroke of her ponderous flukes." Whalers soon learned to use this trait to their advantage; by harpooning a calf, they would lure its mother within range of their deadly harpoons.

Biologists have encountered the same aggressive behavior from cows guarding calves in the lagoons. Their research skiffs have been nearly capsized when they've ventured too close to mothers with calves.

A cow's protectiveness is far from unwarranted. Even with the best of care, calf mortalities run high. Researchers often find calves stranded on the sandbars and banks of the calving lagoons. During the 1980 season alone, nearly 40 calves were found dead in these shallow waters. A study of stranding patterns suggests that almost 75 percent of first-year mortalities occur within a few weeks of birth.

Bulls may use their flippers to try to slow females down to mate (top). Thirteen months later, a baby gray is born (above). Babies have smooth, dark skin free of barnacles.

Visitors to the lagoons often find skeletons on shore. Many calves die in the first few months after birth.

As calves grow, they become playful. They may mimic the breaching or spyhopping behaviors of adults, or invent a few games of their own. Some calves play with the small rubber boats filled with tourists and researchers. A more rambunctious gray may repeatedly bump the vessels from below, using its head as a battering ram. An especially playful adult in San Ignacio Lagoon earned the nickname "Bopper" from whale watchers.

BEHAVIOR IN THE LAGOONS The months spent in the lagoons are times of great activity for cows, bulls and calves. Whale watchers and researchers witness quite an array of gray whale behaviors, some that can be easily explained but others that continue to baffle scientists.

Occasionally, a gray whale extends its head vertically from the sea, as if to get a good look at the sights above the water's surface. Watching a whale raise its head and slowly scan the horizon for 30 seconds or more, it's easy to accept this simple explanation for a behavior called spyhopping. The question still remains about how a 35-ton whale can raise its heavy head out of the water for extended periods. Some researchers propose that the whales support their bodies by planting their flukes on the shallow bottom of the Mexican lagoons. In the deep waters of the open ocean, whales may spyhop using rapid thrusts of their powerful flukes.

No one really knows what motivates a gray whale to breach. A whale will suddenly burst from the water, launching as much as three-fourths of its body into the air before turning onto its side or back and crashing into the sea with an enormous splash. This impressive show of strength may be part of a courtship display, a warning signal to other whales nearby, an attempt to dislodge skin parasites, a gray whale's idea of fun, or perhaps a combination of all of these reasons. Gray whales usually breach two or three times in a row, every 15 seconds or so, but whale watchers report as many as 40 successive breaches. A breaching whale sometimes seems to inspire other whales to breach.

Young gray whales aren't strong swimmers at first and often rest on their mothers' backs or flukes. As they get older, groups of calves play together, mimicking adults and strengthening skills they'll need later in life.

*We don't really know
why whales lift their
30-ton bodies into the
air to breach (top), but it
takes incredible amounts
of energy.*

*Some whales in the
lagoons heft their flukes
into the air and "sail"
along with the breeze
and currents, like the
whale on the left.*

On windy days in Magdalena Bay, a gray whale may raise its
flukes up out of the water and, by catching a strong gust of wind,
"sail" downwind with the breeze, assisted by tidal currents.
Swimming back to its starting place, the whale sets sail again. Grays
also spend a lot of time "body surfing" in the huge waves that break
on the sandbars at the lagoon's entrance. Whale biologists guess
that this behavior may fall within the category of whale "play"—an
activity with no clear function. Simply put, the whales may do it
because it's fun.

On several occasions, gray whales have been seen dragging their
mouths along the silty bottoms of the shallow lagoons, their flukes
sticking up out of the water. They appear to be mimicking their
method of feeding in Arctic seas. However, because the lagoons' silty
bottoms do not support the gray's preferred food species, it's
doubtful that any food gathering results from all the mouthfuls of
sand and silt. Since it's usually calves that behave like this, it may
merely be practice for the months of feeding yet to come.

Do gray whales ever sleep? We don't really know. Those who
observe migrating whales have not seen the swimming whales stop
for long periods of rest. In fact, research shows that migrating gray
whales off the coast of California continue to swim at the same
speed during the night as during the day. An exception to this

"Friendly" whales in the lagoons sometimes approach small boats. Strict guidelines that protect whales from harassment prevent boats from getting too close. But nothing stops a curious whale from coming over for a closer look.

involves mother whales and nursing calves traveling north. They may stop in a sheltered cove or along a protected part of the coastline to nurse and rest. Perhaps the other whales need less sleep during the migration. Grays may indeed travel on "autopilot," resting half of the brain while they swim.

More obvious "sleep" occurs in the southern lagoons, where many visitors comment on the "loglike" appearance of adult whales, mothers and calves. They rest, seeming to sleep, at or just below the surface, occasionally awakening with a start. These "sleeping" whales rise to the surface at eight- or ten-minute intervals for slow breaths of air. Similar behavior is reported far north in the feeding grounds near St. Lawrence Island in the Bering Sea.

SINGING WHALES? Gray whales have voices, although the sounds they produce are very different from our own. Like all other whales, grays lack vocal cords. Biologists think that a gray whale makes sounds by squeezing air through its muscular larynx, or through the pharyngeal pouches near its blowhole. While we can guess how they make the sounds, no one fully understands their purpose.

Scientists have heard just a few gray whale sounds, mostly an assortment of grunts, low frequency rumbles and clicks. Some of these sounds have been compared to the metallic ring of Caribbean steel drums. Grays do not have the rich repertoire of calls heard in the songs of humpbacks.

Using underwater microphones, researchers have identified six distinct types of sounds coming from gray whales in the lagoons. The whales appear to be most vocal when they have gathered together in a small area, when single whales chase cow-calf pairs, when they swim with bottlenose dolphins and when they are on a collision course with skiffs, boats or one another. So far, no signals have been recorded from courting gray whales, although grays are much more vocal in the breeding lagoons than on the feeding grounds or while migrating.

Grays also produce different sounds when confronted with noises from non-living sources. They'll actually alter the structure and timing of their sounds to circumvent noises from boat engines and other underwater sources.

4

THE LONG JOURNEY NORTH

Each spring, gray whales leave their southern breeding lagoons in a remarkably orderly manner. Two distinct but overlapping "pulses" of the northward migration occur. During the first wave, the whales are in transit from February to June and during the second, they travel from March to July. The leaders of the first migrational pulse are the newly impregnated cows. They're followed by the adult bulls, immature cows, and soon, the immature bulls. New mothers and their calves are the sole participants of the second migratory pulse. They usually remain in the lagoons for another month or two before setting out on the long journey north.

NAVIGATING ALONG THE COAST Once outside the lagoons, the whales swim north along the Mexican coast with speed and determination. Some may stop in at other lagoons along the way: San Ignacio Lagoon seems to be a staging area for northward-moving whales.

Exactly how these whales find their way in the nearshore waters of the Pacific remains unclear. Grays are a coastal species, spending most of their time in waters over the continental shelf that lies close to shore. Migrating grays stay roughly in water that's 30 to 40 fathoms deep as they travel along the central California coast. The low-frequency sounds they produce may be used as a primitive "sonar" that determines relative depth in shallow seas. The whales may also use these sounds to communicate with each other, guiding the animals in front or behind as they travel along the narrow, well-defined migratory route.

The whales' acute hearing may also help them discern the sound of wave action along the shore. Or it may help to identify the staccato clicks produced by pistol shrimp in kelp beds or the noises made by fish and other aquatic animals.

Many gray whales may also follow offshore routes over deep water. Many of the southward migrating whales may head due south from Pt. Conception on California's coast, following a diverse track that takes them outside, or among, the Channel Islands.

No one really knows just how well gray whales can see as they swim. It's certain, however, that they swim through regions where underwater visibility is extremely poor. Other senses than vision may help whales navigate. Some scientists propose that the whales rely on some "geographic memory"—an inborn recognition of the distinctive tastes or "scents" of water from particular estuaries, lagoons and river systems—to guide them.

Migrating gray whales often swim in formation just below the surface (below). Mothers and calves, like the pair at left, travel at a slower pace.

Finally, there's recent evidence that magnetism may be leading the way. Experiments with homing pigeons reveal their ability to use the "map" of the Earth's magnetic field. Many birds, and some whales, carry tiny particles of magnetite—a black oxide of iron—in their brains. Like other iron oxides, magnetite particles are strongly affected by magnetic fields. Pods of pilot whales that strand themselves on beaches may have read false clues from the Earth's magnetic field. This would explain why mass strandings of pilot whales consistently occur in areas where the Earth's magnetic fields are anomalous—places like Cape Cod, Massachusetts, and the coasts of north Florida and south Georgia.

While gray whales don't strand en masse, they may share this "map-reading" ability. We suspect that whales learn navigational cues as they mature and are repeatedly exposed to them. Navigation among cetaceans, while extremely difficult to study, is clearly an area where more research is needed.

Although gray whales don't strand in large groups like other kinds of whales, an average of 14 gray whale strandings are reported each year on the west coast of the United States. The frequency of strandings in California, Oregon and Washington is roughly proportional to the length of the coastline of these states. In each of these states, human-related mortality involving animals entangled in gillnets or slashed by boat propellers account for roughly 20 to 25 percent of the strandings.

Gray whales strand along the coast of California more frequently than other large whales.

KILLER WHALES AND GRAY WHALES

Pods of roaming killer whales attack grays in the northeast Pacific.

With the exception of humans, gray whales have few natural enemies. Only one, the killer whale (*Orcinus orca*) poses a threat to the Pacific coast's seasonal migrants.

Killer whales are toothed whales that grow to lengths of 27 to 31 feet. While much smaller than gray whales, their speed, hunting style and voraciousness make them a considerable threat to sea creatures. Traveling in extended family groups called "pods," these sleek predators can chase down and capture salmon and other fishes with relative ease.

Especially dangerous to marine mammals are so-called "transient pods" of killer whales, which differ from the resident, salmon-eating pods of the Pacific Northwest. Transient pods prefer warm-blooded prey—seals, sea lions, dolphins, porpoises and whales. Hunting as a coordinated team, these killer whales often seek out and overcome young calves or yearlings.

Pods attack their victims, chasing them until they are exhausted and drown. Pods may adopt a "code of silence" as they approach prey, thus increasing their element of surprise.

Flukes of grays frequently bear a set of long parallel scars from killer whale teeth. Dead gray whales are occasionally found with huge bites taken out of their mouths, signs of the hunter's preference for the tongue and throat blubber. They may abandon the rest of the carcass.

Reports exist of grays so paralyzed with fear that they turn over on their backs instead of fleeing or fighting the killer whales. Yet mothers may vigorously defend their calves. One eyewitness account tells of a female gray fending off several killers, using her flipper to hold her calf up out of the water. Mothers with calves may also take refuge in kelp beds or among nearshore rocks to escape killer whale pods.

Killer whales may attack mothers and calves.

Killer whale teeth scarred this gray's fluke.

THE WHALES OF SUMMER Not all gray whales migrate all the way from the Arctic to Baja California and back. Grays have been seen during the summer at several locations along the way. This could be related to the increasing number of grays in our waters. As more whales re-populate the seas, the whales expand their range into areas rich with their preferred food.

In the summer, grays have lingered in the Gulf of the Farallones, off the coast of northern California and near Westport, Washington. As many as 30 grays have been counted off the central Oregon coast between the Alsea River and Cape Foulweather. Nearly a third of the animals are calves and a sizeable number are yearlings. Since most of the feeding takes place in fairly deep water, biologists have yet to determine exactly what Oregon's summer whales are eating. But regardless of what they're feeding on, the whales reap benefits from summering over. They may be conserving energy by shortening the length of their migration. They're also able to begin feeding much earlier in the summer and continue feeding much later into the fall.

Between 40 and 50 grays are also regularly sighted each summer along the outer coast of Vancouver Island, British Columbia. Whales in this region are apparently feeding on small mysid shrimp, *Holmesimysis sculpta* and *Neomysis rayii*, which swarm in large numbers close to the bottom in the feeding areas. They also seem to be feeding on amphipods sucked out of the mud. By comparing photographs of individual whales taken over time, one whale biologist determined that at least one of these whales remained off the island's coast throughout the summer and returned several years in a row. The longest recorded stay of a gray along the island's coast was seven months. This animal was seen fairly often between April and October during the years of study.

Low tide reveals shallow pits excavated by a feeding gray whale on the west coast of Vancouver Island.

MIGRATORY PATHS These obvious exceptions to the long-distance rule have led scientists to reconsider the evolution of the gray whale's current migratory path. Changes in the Earth's climate over the last 20,000 years, they reason, may have had dramatic effects on the movements of whales at different times.

Approximately 18,000 years ago, when glaciers covered the North American continent to their maximum extent, sea levels were about 400 feet lower than they are today. A wide strip of land, the Bering land bridge, joined the continents of North America and Asia. Some scientists believe that the drop in sea level made more shallow feeding grounds accessible to the bottom-feeding gray whales than ever before. The shallow waters surrounding the land we now call Baja California may have been good feeding grounds for grays. Only as the melting glaciers receded and the sea level rose were the whales required to journey farther afield in search of food.

This line of reasoning contradicts another, perhaps more accurate view, which maintains that the submerged continental shelves of land along the Pacific coast of North America were narrower 18,000 years ago. Therefore, gray whales would have had

Biologists have identified gray whales summering off Vancouver Island that seem to return to the same feeding areas each year. Research continues into their diving behavior and food preferences.

substantially less area in which to feed. Fewer feeding grounds would mean fewer whales.

According to this second view, rising sea levels, which made the low-lying Bering land bridge disappear, gave gray whales access to their current rich and extensive feeding grounds in the Bering and Chukchi seas.

The migratory paths of gray whales continue to evolve. A few animals even venture into the waters of the Canadian Arctic. Yet exploration so far north can be dangerous for the whales. Pack ice, always present at these latitudes in summer, expands and thickens rapidly once temperatures plummet in late fall. Any lingering whales may become trapped by the ice.

As far as we can tell, this is how three young grays became trapped in the ice 10 miles east of Barrow, Alaska in October, 1988. Perhaps these whales—the smallest a nine-month-old juvenile born that year and the largest a 3½-year-old, 35-foot whale—were so inexperienced and intent on feeding that they failed to notice the ice that threatened to imprison them. When discovered by an Inuit hunter, the whales were completely surrounded by ice.

In earlier years, such a find would have been put to good use by the Inuit, their families and their sled dogs. The whales would have met the Inuits' needs throughout the long winter. But this time the Inuit worked hard to keep the whales alive. The hunter and his fellow villagers used chainsaws to cut the ice, creating a line of breathing holes that led in the direction of open water, five miles away. Water circulation pumps kept the holes from re-freezing during the 16-hour nights.

News personnel from around the world rushed to Barrow to report on the fate of the three captive whales. On October 15, a decision was reached to attempt a rescue, rather than to let nature take its course. And as word of the trapped whales spread, other help arrived. Attempts to bring in a helicopter-hoverbarge failed. Following a request from the State Department, two massive Soviet

Two young gray whales trapped in the ice surface to breathe in holes cut by Inuit villagers.

icebreakers were dispatched. The whales appeared energized, even entering new holes before the chainsaws had finished the opening. De-icers placed in the water attracted the whales' attention, overcoming their hesitancy to swim beneath the ice to new holes. The smallest whale disappeared on October 21, perhaps unable to navigate beneath the ice to reach the new holes with its companions. A Soviet icebreaker, the 518-foot *Vladimir Arseniev*, eventually succeeded in breaking the ice and leading the whales to open water on October 28.

It remains unclear whether the other two whales survived to reach safety in the Bering Strait and pass southward. The weather was clear and ice conditions looked favorable. Perhaps even more remarkable than the whales' release from the ice was the incredible media attention their plight commanded.

Three gray whales became trapped in pack ice when they stayed too long or ventured too far north in their feeding grounds, shown in the map below. One died, and the long-term fate of the other two is unknown.

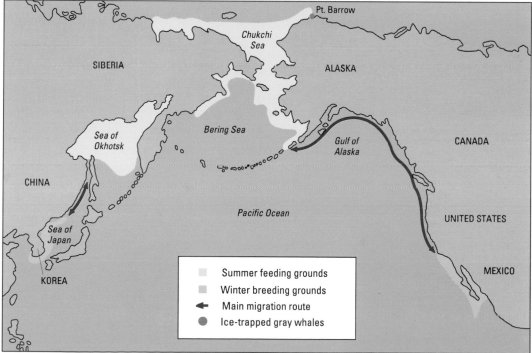

SWIMMING, BREATHING AND DIVING To successfully complete the journey between feeding and breeding grounds, gray whales must be steady swimmers, covering nearly a hundred miles in a day. At this rate, they can complete the southward journey from Unimak Pass in Alaska to Baja California in an average of 55 days. Whales have been clocked at slightly slower swimming speeds on their journeys north. They may be pacing themselves, spending as little energy as possible, or they may be feeding along the way. Mothers with calves move much slower.

A gray whale typically breathes three to five times in a row, 10 to 20 seconds apart, closing its paired blowholes to seal off its lungs between breaths. Then it dives for three to seven minutes, or, if necessary, remains beneath the sea for up to 20 minutes. Returning to the surface from a depth of about 200 feet, it expels air with an audible "whoosh" and a heart-shaped spout, or "blow", up to 15 feet high. This blow is not really the gushing fountain of water depicted in cartoons. While the spout *does* contain droplets of sea water carried aloft, it's mostly made up of condensation created when

You can tell a gray whale by its bushy heart-shaped blow, formed by twin nostrils.

the whale's warm, vaporous breath meets the cool ocean air. Oil droplets and small amounts of mucus mixed in with the vapor give the spout a distinctive, fishy odor, but only when the whale has recently been feeding. Fountain or not, this blast of warm, wet air is impressive. Roughly 100 gallons of air, enough to fill two oil drums, are expelled from the gray whale's blowhole every time it exhales. Nearly 90 percent of this air is forced out in less than one second.

Grays dive to feed in fairly shallow water, usually less than 300 feet, and can stay down as long as 20 minutes. The average dive lasts 5 minutes.

5

ON THE FEEDING GROUNDS

By early summer, most gray whales have arrived at their feeding grounds, an area covering approximately 35,000 square miles in the northern and western Bering, Chukchi and Beaufort seas. Life in these waters, particularly those of the Bering Sea, is among the world's most abundant. Great schools of herring, cod, salmon, pollock and other commercially valuable fishes sweep through the bitterly cold seas, passing over a silty and sandy seafloor littered with sea stars, urchins, clams, anemones and crabs and a host of other invertebrates.

Gray whales share their rich feeding grounds with more than fishes and invertebrates. As they forage, the grays are joined by smaller marine mammals—killer whales, white whales, harbor porpoises, several kinds of seals, Steller sea lions and walruses. Many seabirds also reap the seasonal harvest of marine life.

During seven months of migrating and socializing in the lagoons of Baja California, gray whales survive almost entirely on fat reserves acquired during the previous summer's stay at the feeding grounds. Some of the whales may eat small amounts along the way, breaking their fasts with a few mouthfuls of krill or quick gulps of anchovies or other small baitfish.

In the Arctic feeding grounds, grays again seem to segregate in much the same way they do in the lagoons, with mothers and calves moving farther north into the Chukchi Sea, north of the major feeding areas. This isolation may help them elude hunting killer whales.

Once in the Bering Sea, it's time for the whales to feast. Over the next five months on the feeding grounds, the grays will gain back an estimated 16 to 30 percent of their total body weight. In the process, they'll restore their blubber layer and interior body fat. Blubber and fat reserves are an energy resource that will help them complete the southward leg of their journey, sustain them in the Mexican lagoons and nurture them as they travel north again to feed.

A feeding gray whale (right) has just scooped up a mouthful of mud loaded with small amphipods, its preferred food (below). Grays may also feed on mud-dwelling ghost shrimp in a few areas (bottom).

SATISFYING A WHALE OF AN APPETITE Charles Scammon wrote of gray whales returning to the surface of the Bering Sea, their "head and lips besmeared with the dark ooze from the depths below." Incorrectly assuming that the whales were feeding on buried shellfish, his fellow whalers added "mussel digger" to the whale's already lengthy list of nicknames.

The gray whale is the only baleen whale that regularly feeds on bottom-dwelling animals, a feeding strategy that lets the gray avoid

competition with other whale species. However, its favored food is not the mussel or, for that matter, any other form of mollusc. By studying the food items from the stomachs of captured gray whales, we've learned that amphipods are the whales' primary source of nourishment. Related to crabs, shrimp and other crustaceans, the 3,600 species of the order Amphipoda have evolved to fill a wide range of ecological niches. Most are small—anywhere from one-third of an inch to one inch in length. Most have made their home in the marine environment, although some live on land. Sand-hoppers (*Gammarus* sp.), or beach fleas as they're commonly known, are amphipods frequently found on many coastal beaches.

Amphipods from four separate families account for as much as 90 percent of the food found in the stomachs of captured gray whales. Tube-building amphipods in the family Ampeliscidae that live in dense colonies or "mats" on the seafloor are the most abundant. These tube dwellers build their houses out of small sand grains. Secure in their homes, they snare tiny plankton and other small bits of food from the seafloor. In some parts of the Bering Sea, these seafloor colonies may contain as many as 3,000 individual amphipods per square foot.

Members of the three other amphipod families, Atylidae, Lysianassidae and Haustoriidae, are scavengers. Unlike the Ampeliscidae, which remain in their tubes year-round, these animals wander freely in search of food. Many feed on the animals attached to the strawlike tubes of the Ampeliscidae. Others, particularly amphipods of the genera *Atylus* and *Anonyx*, feed on pieces of sponges, worms and other food left behind by foraging grays.

Compared with the sperm whale, which hunts to depths of 3,000 feet or more, and other deep-diving species of whales, most

As a feeding whale rises off the bottom, it releases a mouthful of mud through its comblike baleen. The food gets trapped on the baleen and scraped off by the whale's large tongue.

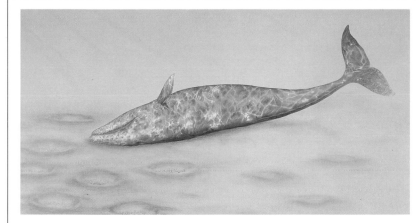

A feeding gray whale swims on its side to suck mud off the bottom, creating a 7-foot-long pit that roughly corresponds to the size of one side of the whale's closed mouth.

grays feed in fairly shallow water. They suck up mud from the seafloor, generally less than 165 feet deep in the Bering Sea and 225 feet deep in the Chukchi Sea. However, watching whales as they feed in the cold, murky and current-swept northern seas is a difficult task, even at these depths. As a result, few high-quality underwater films or photographs of feeding whales existed until recently, when actively feeding grays were filmed at Pachena Bay near Bamfield on Vancouver Island.

Early observers of gray whales believed that the "mussel digger" behaved much like an underwater power shovel, scooping up great mouthfuls of sand and silt in its massive lower jaw. They abandoned this idea after learning that amphipods and other animals fed on by the whales were found in a layer of sediment less than an inch deep. Extensive plowing of the bottom would be unnecessary, and might even damage the whale's easily scratched skin.

Grays draw in their prey using suction. When feeding, a whale swims parallel to the seafloor, slowly turning its body and bringing the side of its mouth within a few inches of the bottom. Because most gray whales bear fewer barnacles and more skin abrasions on the right sides of their heads, some whales may be "righthanded," while others appear to favor their left side.

A feeding whale opens it mouth slightly as it retracts its huge tongue, which weighs around 2,500 pounds. The resulting suction draws in sediment from the bottom and jets it through the baleen filter on the other side of the animal's mouth. Amphipods and other morsels are trapped by the baleen. Sand and mud shoot out in great plumes, visible from any aircraft or boats in the vicinity of the surfacing whale. The whale then uses its tongue to push the food back into its narrow throat, and swallows.

During its five-month feast on the feeding grounds, an adult gray whale will swallow what has been conservatively measured at around 67 tons of food. Because the amphipod populations in many parts of the Bering and Chukchi seas are widely dispersed (in some places, a square foot of Bering Sea sediment may yield less than half an ounce of amphipods), a single whale may sift through nearly 100 acres of bottom sediment before it heads south in the fall.

GRAY WHALE FEEDING GROUNDS As you can imagine, the bottom is battered wherever the whales feed. Suction-feeding leaves huge pits in the seafloor, creating what one researcher has described as "mortar-pocked battlefields from an old John Wayne movie." In some areas of the Bering, Chukchi and Beaufort seas, recently formed pits scar over 40 percent of the bottom.

Grays disturb their feeding grounds more than any other mammal, even elephants, although areas where whales feed re-colonize and recover very rapidly. Yet while the bottom may look like a battlefield, scientists believe that life on the seafloor may actually benefit from the gray whales' feeding activities. Far from stripping the bottom of all life, the whales may open up new areas for re-colonization, indirectly helping marine life proliferate on the seafloor. Gray whales may be seeding the area with juvenile amphi-pods—animals small enough to pass through the whales' baleen sieve. The escapees quickly re-establish themselves on the seafloor, creating new colonies of tube-dwelling amphipods. As the colonies grow, other invertebrates move into this freshly created habitat.

Feeding gray whales also tend to stir up nutrients that have previously settled to the bottom. Suspended again in the water column, the nutrients stimulate the growth of plankton, a primary food source for tube-dwelling amphipods and other invertebrates. Accidental farmers, the gray whales tend to their invertebrate "crops" in one final way: they prevent mud, naturally discharged into the Bering Sea by the Yukon and other large Alaskan rivers, from smothering the sandy habitat of the amphipods. Whenever the feeding whales spew sediment into the water, heavy sand and grit

soon sinks to the bottom, while lighter weight particles of clay and fine silt are carried by water currents away from the feeding grounds. Whale researchers estimate that a minimum of 156 million tons of sediment is sifted by gray whales in the Bering Sea every year. This is nearly three times the amount of mud-bearing sediment that the Yukon River discharges each year into the same body of water.

Feeding gray whales also benefit several species of seabirds, which trail behind the surfacing whales and pick up discarded or injured prey. Whale followers include glaucous gulls, black-legged kittiwakes, auklets and phalaropes.

THE JOURNEY BEGINS AGAIN   As summer draws to a close, the days shorten, and the air and water in the Bering Sea begin to chill. Out on the Chukchi Sea, water at the surface turns into solid ice. Environmental signals cue the whales that it's time to swim south again.

Grays leave their summer feeding grounds in the same order they left the breeding lagoons five months or so ago. First to head south are the pregnant cows. They're followed by the adult bulls. Immature bulls and cows come next, bringing up the rear. Some juveniles may actually head south but will turn back when they encounter northbound adults off California and return north with them.

Unlike the lean animals that left the Mexican lagoons, the southbound whales bear thick layers of fat. Their newly restored fat reserves will sustain them until they return to these northern seas.

Mud plumes mark the path of a feeding gray whale. Northern seabirds like red phalaropes (above), feed on the leftover food in the plumes.

6

GRAY WHALES IN MONTEREY BAY

As they travel from their icy feeding grounds to the warmer breeding lagoons and back gray whales, especially juveniles, may meander into larger bays along the way, including Monterey Bay on the central coast of California. Monterey has long held a reputation as a place for whales. "It is impossible either to describe the number of whales with which we were surrounded, or their familiarity. They blowed every half a minute within half a pistol shot from our frigates," wrote Jean François de Galaup de La Pérouse in September 1786, one of the earliest explorers of Monterey Bay. La Pérouse's observations probably referred to humpbacks and were later repeated by the English explorer Sir George Simpson. "A favorite resort of the fish," declared Simpson in his book, *Narrative of a Voyage to California Ports in 1840-1842*, written after his close encounters with Monterey's whales.

As years passed, the nature of peoples' encounters with whales changed. Shore whaling stations soon sprang up around Monterey Bay, and the gray whale became more of a commodity and less of a creature of wonder. "The number of whale bones on the beach is astonishing—the beach is white with them," recalled W.H. Brewer, a chronicler of Monterey life in the 1860s.

Over the last 20 years, Monterey's gray whales have lured a different kind of person—one more eager to watch the spectacular offshore migration than to take whales from it. The owners of Monterey's small fleet of sportfishing boats have been quick to assist these new arrivals. In winters past, the fishermen might have spent December and January repairing their boats and waiting for fishing season to start again. But now, as Christmas approaches, these enterprising souls simply hang out new shingles, replacing their "Fishing Trip" placards with ones that read "Whale Watching Cruise Today."

The whale watching phenomenon for grays began modestly enough in 1955, when a single boat would set out from San Diego, on California's southern shore. Now more than 300 charter vessels a year are offering whale watching cruises off the Pacific coast. Over a dozen of these boats make Monterey Bay their home port. Revenues from whale watching have steadily grown. In a single year, whale watching brought in $6 million in California and another $4.5 to $6 million in Oregon, Washington, British Columbia and Alaska. At the same time, sales of whale-related items such as T-shirts, posters and guidebooks brought in at least $3.5 million.

A gray whale surfacing in a kelp bed may be feeding on shrimplike mysid swarms, but not on the kelp itself. Grays rarely feed off the coast of central and southern California.

A Cetacean Parade Each year as Christmas approaches, so do the gray whales. While a few individuals, presumably pregnant cows, are usually sighted by Monterey fishermen and boaters in mid-November, the southbound grays don't appear in numbers until mid-December. The first major migratory pulse hits the bay around Christmas. Within weeks, as many as 200 whales a day can be counted by area whale watchers. These newcomers include adult bulls and immature males and females. Ordinarily they travel in pods of one to four animals, but during the peak of the migration, anywhere from January 7 to 17, it's possible to find pods of 12 to 15 gray whales.

Most grays migrate south across the bay from the Davenport area in Santa Cruz County, approaching the shore in Monterey County near Point Pinos or Cypress Point. The migrants follow a corridor, which lies along the western outer edge of the bay, roughly 11 to 14 miles west of Moss Landing. Grays are rare in the northeastern section of the bay and any sightings from shore at places such as Pajaro Dunes are quite noteworthy.

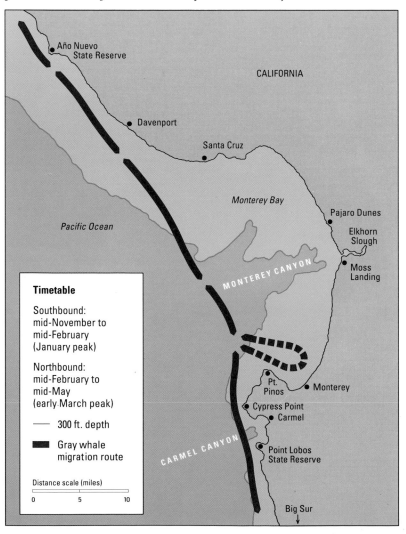

Año Nuevo
State Reserve

CALIFORNIA

Davenport

Santa Cruz

Monterey Bay

Pajaro Dunes

Pacific Ocean

Elkhorn
Slough

MONTEREY CANYON

Moss
Landing

Timetable

Southbound:
mid-November to
mid-February
(January peak)

Northbound:
mid-February to
mid-May
(early March peak)

—— 300 ft. depth

■■■ Gray whale
migration route

Distance scale (miles)

0   5   10

Pt.
Pinos   Monterey

Cypress Point
Carmel

Point Lobos
State Reserve

CARMEL CANYON

Big Sur
↓

Gray whales leave their main migration route about 14 miles west of Moss Landing to wander into Monterey Bay during both their northward and southward migrations. They rarely enter the northeast part of the bay, but can sometimes be seen from shore from Moss Landing south to Monterey.

Occasionally, the whales will turn left at Point Pinos, steering for the comparatively calm water inside the bay. We don't know why the whales meander, but these seemingly misdirected individuals, both adults and juveniles, may swim well into the bay before adjusting their courses, looping back and heading south again along the coast.

The main southward migration continues throughout January, with a gradual decline in the number of grays passing through. The last of the stragglers are usually seen in mid-February. Since the first migrants swimming north are also sighted in February, it's not uncommon to see grays traveling through the bay in both directions during this month. Seeing the congestion caused by whales as they approach Point Pinos from several directions, whale researchers call this prominent headland "Piccadilly Circus for Grays."

The northbound migration usually peaks in Monterey Bay during the first week or two of March. Sightings decline rapidly in April, with reports of small numbers of whales continuing through mid-May and occasionally late into the month. During the north-bound migration, most whales seem to move away from shore after passing Cypress Point, frequently passing three to five miles or more west of Point Pinos. Mothers with their calves tend to follow the shoreline more closely, actually entering the inner reaches of the bay. They're often seen from mid-April through mid-May, hugging the submerged kelp forests that fringe the shore. Protective gray whale mothers make sure that their calves swim close. Cows and calves may rest or nurse in sheltered places en route, and, as you might expect, the pace of these pairs is much slower than that of the other travelers.

Killer whale attacks, although rare, are usually reported during this period. Most beached carcasses, whether dead from attacks or other causes, are found here from March to May. White sharks have been seen feeding on floating dead grays.

Many whale watchers try to estimate the number of grays in a traveling pod by counting the blows, backs and flukes of sounding whales.

WHALING ALONG THE MONTEREY COAST

Monterey's shore whaling companies are long gone, but the houses and shacks where whalers once worked remain as relics from a previous era.

Known to Monterey residents as the First Brick House, Captain J.P. Davenport's home was purchased by the State of California in 1979. Rehabilitated, it's a part of Monterey State Historic Park. In this same park stands the Old Whaling Station, an attractive two-story building of stucco and wood that housed the Portuguese whalers who worked for Davenport. Passing whales, the story goes, could easily be spotted from windows on the second floor. Cobbles in the sidewalk in front of the station were made from the vertebrae of captured whales.

Whale-bone artifacts are also in evidence at another Monterey landmark, California's First Theatre, also known as the Jenny Lind. Long ago, whale ribs were installed in an arch over the theater's main entrance, along with four whale vertebrae that served as handrail supports for the theater's front steps. The bones are still there today.

Perhaps the most impressive holdover from the heyday of gray whaling is the restored shore whaling station at Point Lobos on Carmel Bay. Visiting this historic site, now a favorite attraction at Point Lobos State Reserve, it's easy to let Charles Scammon's vivid description of the station in the 1870s fill the mind's eye:

"Under a precipitous bluff, close to the water's edge, is the station. . . . Nearby are the try-works, sending forth volumes of thick, black smoke from the scrap-fire under the steaming cauldrons of boiling oil. A little to one side is the primitive storehouse, covered with cypress boughs. Boats are hanging from davits, some resting on the quay, while others, fully equipped, swing at their moorings in the bay. Seaward, on the crest of a cone-shaped hill, stands the signal pole of the lookout station. Add to this the cutting at the shapeless and half-putrid mass of a mutilated whale, together with the men shouting and heaving on the capstans, the screaming of gulls and other sea-fowl, mingled with the noise of the surf above the shores, and we have a picture of the general life at a California coast-whaling station."

Scammon described whaling at Carmel Bay, now called Whaler's Cove at Point Lobos State Reserve.

BEHAVIOR IN THE BAY During both northbound and southbound migrations, whale watchers in Monterey Bay and other locations along the coast have ample opportunities to see gray whales in action. They watch firsthand many of the same behaviors observed in the breeding lagoons of Mexico. Breaching is more common than spyhopping, which is rare. Lucky whale watchers have seen courtship in calm seas from mid-January on, and throughout the northbound migration. Mating may occur close to shore, or away from the shore over deeper water where it appears to rouse the curiosity of California sea lions and Pacific white-sided dolphins. Courting grays may stop swimming and float belly up at the surface, especially when closely attended by Risso's dolphins. No one really knows why.

The first newborn gray whale in Monterey Bay was observed in January, 1973. Since then, births in or near Monterey Bay have been reported each January. The calves probably survive, since so far only one beach-washed carcass of a calf has been found in the bay. Perhaps the calves die along the way, south of Monterey.

Whales occasionally feed in the bay, usually during the north-ward migration. Marine biologists in small aircraft once watched grays skim the surface and gulp anchovies or other schooling fishes. Others have happened upon whales feeding within kelp beds, perhaps on swarms of tiny mysid shrimps. Unusually abundant swarms of krill at the bay's surface in spring also appear to attract opportunistic feedings by gray whales, although very infrequently. The absence of gray whale feces during their migration through this area gives us indirect evidence that they rarely feed here.

Grays have actually strayed into the harbor at Moss Landing, even into the shallow water of Elkhorn Slough, possibly in search of prey. A few hangers-on, usually small whales, have been sighted now and then during the summer in the bay and nearby seas. They may be snacking on mats of the tube-dwelling worm *Diopatra* and other species found there, even though their favorite species of tube-dwelling amphipod doesn't live in the bay.

Grays aren't the only whales to watch in the bay. Overlapping with the last of the grays in late April and early May, northbound humpback whales may pass by. Blue whales arrive in the bay in late June or July in most years, with frequent sightings through October.

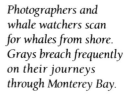

Photographers and whale watchers scan for whales from shore. Grays breach frequently on their journeys through Monterey Bay.

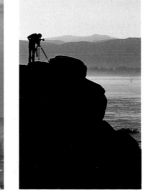

COUNTING WHALES

Whale biologists have taken advantage of the Monterey peninsula's abundance of shore lookouts and the nearness of migrating whales to get an accurate count of gray whales. Each fall from 1966 to 1977, and at approximately five-year intervals since then, biologists with the National Marine Mammal Laboratory of the National Oceanic and Atmospheric Administration set up camp first at Yankee Point and later at Granite Canyon. From these natural vantage points high over the waves, the researchers watched with binoculars and scopes, recording the numbers of whales passing the field stations by day. From the data they collected from 10 daylight hours, other scientists extrapolated the total number of animals, around 15,600, that passed the station day and night. (Today, gray whales number more than 21,000.)

In 1977, another team using similar field observation methods counted the populations of whales that traveled north each spring through Unimak Pass, in the eastern Aleutian Islands of Alaska. They used the number of whales counted during daylight hours to estimate that about 17,000 whales traveled that way day and night.

Surveys both in California and Alaska were conducted only during daylight hours, when visibility was unimpeded by rain or fog. Therefore, the numbers of whales obtained from both surveys represented only those whales that could be seen and counted by day. To determine the actual number of whales migrating along the coast, it was assumed that approximately the same number of whales swam past the research stations by night.

But did the whales in fact travel by night and day? To answer that question, two researchers attached battery-powered devices called "radio tags" to the backs of nine gray whales as they swam along the central California coast.

Getting close enough to the whales to attach the radio tags could have been a problem. However, researchers developed an ingenious method for overcoming this obstacle: they used a specially constructed crossbow to fire aluminum arrows fitted with barbed radio tags at the whales. Upon impact with the whale, the tag separated from its arrow, leaving only the tag's antennae protruding from the skin. Surprisingly, this seemed to barely bother the whales. Securely fastened in the skin and blubber, the radio tags emitted electronic signals that could be picked up by receiving systems on board a small vessel that followed the whales.

By interpreting the electronic signals transmitted by the radio tags, the researchers could monitor the whales' movements and establish their nocturnal behavior. From these data, scientists could now say with certainty that migrating gray whales traveled at the same speed both day and night. The original daytime census figures compiled by the Monterey peninsula team could be extrapolated with accuracy to include those animals that slipped by in darkness.

Biologists radio-tagged grays to study swimming speed, routes and night travel.

Two grays sound in Carmel Bay (above), once the site of an active whaling station, now a popular spot for whale watchers.

"Footprints" (left) tip watchers off to a whale just below the surface.

WATCHING WHALES Getting close to gray whales does not always involve boarding a boat. The bluffs and headlands of the Monterey peninsula and nearby Santa Cruz provide some of the best vantage points to see these ambitious swimmers. Their blows are clearly visible to the naked eye. A powerful pair of binoculars or a high-powered telescope bring backs and flukes into viewing range. Particularly popular lookouts along the central coast include the Davenport Bluffs, Point Pinos, Cypress Point and south across

Carmel Bay at Point Lobos State Reserve. South of Point Lobos the vast majority of whales pass within a mile of shore off Big Sur. Roadside pullouts along the entire Coast Highway leading south through Big Sur are excellent places to observe the flukes and spouts of Monterey's visiting giants.

THREATS TO GRAY WHALES While gray whales are fully protected by law in Monterey Bay and other U.S. waters, they still face many threats. Gillnets set along the coast of southern California entangle grays as well as other marine mammals. Many entrapped whales have been liberated but almost always at great risk to the divers and volunteers involved.

Oil spills seem to pose only an indirect threat to gray whales. Grays traditionally migrate through areas containing natural oil seeps in the Santa Barbara Channel without any apparent harm. And there doesn't seem to be any evidence of gray whales dying as a result of recent big oil spills, such as the Santa Barbara oil platform spill in 1969 or the 1989 *Exxon Valdez* tanker spill in Prince William Sound. Gray whales are not feeding when they pass through these waters. If a big spill should occur in the Bering or Chukchi seas on the gray whales' feeding grounds, however, the contamination of their prey in the top layers of the seafloor could be serious.

Are gray whales affected by manmade noises? Experiments reveal that they do seem to go out of their way to avoid simulated sounds of oil-drilling and associated activities. Their offshore route through the Channel Islands off southern California may have developed as ship traffic and noise levels increased. Many

Threats to gray whales include pollution and entanglement in set gillnets. Divers can sometimes free the whales but at great personal risk.

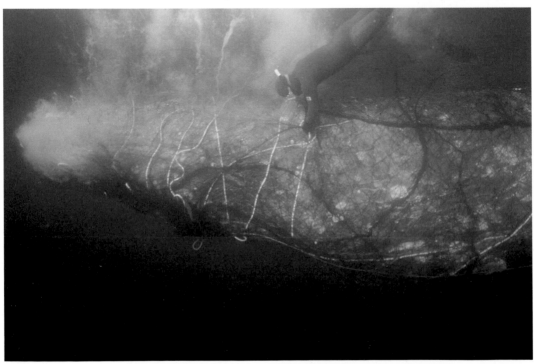

whales now seem to follow this route, with the rest following the mainland coastline.

Industrial activities in the whales' breeding lagoons in Baja California pose a potential threat to the whales. A substantial salt extraction and exportation industry currently exists in Scammon's Lagoon. Any industrial expansion and added barge traffic could harm the gray whales. In the same way, tapping oil reserves under or near the lagoons might be detrimental.

Other threats to gray whales include marina development to house recreational boats in the lagoons. Too much boat traffic could disturb the grays during a critical time in their breeding cycle. Despite these potential problems, the Mexican government has taken great steps to protect gray whales and other marine mammals, like northern elephant seals and Guadalupe fur seals.

GRAY WHALE RESEARCH We still have much to learn about the lives of gray whales. Most of what we understand comes from ongoing studies in the field. Building on this foundation of knowledge, efforts to study, protect and make others aware of gray whales will ensure that these long-distance travelers will grace our coasts for generations to come.

As biologists continue to study these long-distance travelers, we hope to learn more about their mysterious life history.

INDEX